I0796858

UNOFFICIAL & UNAUTHORISED

Cookin' 9 to 5

DOLLY

UNOFFICIAL & UNAUTHORISED

Cookin' 9 to 5

60 RECIPES INSPIRED BY
☆ DOLLY PARTON ☆

First published in Great Britain
in 2025 by Hamlyn, an imprint of
Octopus Publishing Group Ltd
Carmelite House
50 Victoria Embankment
London EC4Y 0DZ
www.octopusbooks.co.uk
www.octopusbooksusa.com

An Hachette UK Company
www.hachette.co.uk

The authorized representative in the EEA is Hachette Ireland, 8 Castlecourt Centre, Dublin 15, D15 XTP3, Ireland (email: info@hbgi.ie)

Distributed in the US by
Hachette Book Group
1290 Avenue of the Americas,
4th and 5th Floors
New York, NY 10104

Distributed in Canada by
Canadian Manda Group
664 Annette St., Toronto, Ontario,
Canada M6S 2C8

ISBN: 978-0-600-63966-4
eISBN: 978-0-600-63967-1

A CIP catalogue record for this book is available from the British Library.

Printed and bound in China.

10 9 8 7 6 5 4 3 2 1

Commissioning Editor: Isabel Jessop
Production Manager: Caroline Alberti

With thanks to Dolly consultants Caroline, Kate and Zeba

Sources: p.12 *The Standard* 5 April 2012; p.21 *Out Magazine* 21 November 2019; p.34 *Southern Living* 2014; p.40 *ABC News* 11 November 2019; p.42 *Entertainment Tonight* 8 June 2016; p.47 @dollyparton on X 14 March 2022; p.58 *The Howard Stern Show* November 2023; p.80 *Wired* 5 October 2020; p.82 *Today* 23 September 2024; p.101 *The Standard* 5 April 2012

Some of this material has previously appeared in other Hamlyn All Colour Cookbooks.

☆ CONTENTS ☆

☆ COOKING NOTES ☆

Standard level spoon measurements are used in all recipes.

1 tablespoon = one 15 ml spoon

1 teaspoon = one 5 ml spoon

Both imperial and metric measurements have been given in all recipes. Use one set of measurements only and not a mixture of both.

Eggs should be medium unless otherwise stated. The Department of Health advises that eggs should not be consumed raw. This book contains dishes made with raw or lightly cooked eggs. It is prudent for more vulnerable people such as pregnant and nursing mothers, invalids, the elderly, babies and young children to avoid uncooked or lightly cooked dishes made with eggs. Once prepared these dishes should be kept refrigerated and used promptly.

Milk should be full fat unless otherwise stated.

Fresh herbs should be used unless otherwise stated. If unavailable use dried herbs as an alternative but halve the quantities stated.

Ovens should be preheated to the specific temperature – if using a fan-assisted oven, follow manufacturer's instructions for adjusting the time and the temperature.

Pepper should be freshly ground black pepper unless otherwise stated.

This book includes dishes made with nuts and nut derivatives. It is advisable for those with known allergic reactions to nuts and nut derivatives and those who may be potentially vulnerable to these allergies, such as pregnant and nursing mothers, the elderly, babies and children, to avoid dishes made with nuts and nut oils. It is also prudent to check the labels of pre-prepared ingredients for the possible inclusion of nut derivatives.

Vegetarians should look for the 'V' symbol on a cheese to ensure it is made with vegetarian rennet.

Introduction

Well, hey there, look who it is! Prepare to kick up your heels with these recipes that celebrate Dolly's life and lyrics. You'll find yourself a-hooting and a-hollering as you partner with the Queen of Country's music on a fabulously foodie adventure. If you've been working 9 to 5 and you're all out of mealtime inspiration, this book will transform your culinary mindset – it's gonna be less Here You Come Again and more I Will Always Love You! Fun facts about Dolly are also sprinkled throughout to add some extra homestyle charm.

Each recipe has simple, step-by-step instructions to follow, with ideas for Breakfast, Lunch, Dinner and Dessert, along with a Drinks section that includes cocktails and non-alcoholic 'mocktails' so you can pour your own cup of ambition. There's even some (song)writing space at the end of the book for your own notes. So, whether this is your first rodeo, or you're an old cooking hand, let's get this show on the road!

Breakfast

OATS Of Many Colours

SERVES 4 | PREP: 10mins | COOKING TIME: 15mins

Dolly wrote the song 'My Coat of Many Colours' about a patchwork coat that her mama made for her from scraps of cloth, and which the other children teased her about in school. These oats can come in many colours so adapt them to fit whatever fruit you have – no waste, no judgement – just ingenuity and talent!

OATS OF MANY COLOURS

☆ INGREDIENTS ☆

500g (1lb) eating apples, peeled, cored and roughly chopped

½ teaspoon ground mixed spice

½ teaspoon ground ginger

5 tablespoons soft brown sugar

8 tablespoons water

600ml (1 pint) milk

150g (5oz) porridge oats

☆ METHOD ☆

1. Place the apples in a medium, heavy-based saucepan with the spices, 3 tablespoons of the sugar and the measured water. Bring to the boil, then reduce the heat to a simmer. Cover and simmer over a very gentle heat for 4–5 minutes, stirring occasionally, until the apples are soft yet still retaining some of their shape.
2. Bring the milk and remaining sugar to the boil, stirring occasionally. Remove from the heat and add the porridge oats. Stir well, then return to a low heat, stirring continuously for 4–5 minutes until the porridge has thickened.
3. Stir half the apple mixture through the porridge until well mixed, then ladle into 4 warmed serving bowls. Spoon over the remaining apple mixture.
4. For hot-pink, swirled porridge, mash 250g (8oz) fresh raspberries with 1 teaspoon golden caster sugar. Make up the porridge following the method above, then remove from the heat and spoon in the mashed raspberries. Using 1–2 stirs only, swirl the raspberries into the porridge before serving.

Rhinestone · PANCAKES ·

SERVES 4 | PREP: 10mins | COOKING TIME: 12–15mins

Time to cook up a breakfast that'll look as good on the plate as it'll feel in your belly! Transfer the pancakes to a baking sheet as you make them and keep warm in a low oven until they're all ready to eat. The soft blueberry compote that tops these pancakes also tastes delicious over yogurt or with granola.

• FUN FACT •

Dolly's famous one-liner, "It costs a lot of money to look this cheap," was in response to critics of her rhinestone-encrusted style. She doubled down on them though, even putting them in the subtitle of her book, *Behind the Seams: My Life in Rhinestones.*

RHINESTONE PANCAKES

☆ INGREDIENTS ☆

FOR THE BUTTERMILK PANCAKES

125g (4oz) plain flour
pinch of salt
1 teaspoon baking powder
200ml (7fl oz) buttermilk
1 egg
1 tablespoon vegetable oil
crème fraîche, to serve (optional)

FOR THE VANILLA BLUEBERRIES

250 g (8 oz) blueberries
2 tablespoons freshly squeezed orange juice
1–2 tablespoons vanilla sugar, to taste
vegetable oil, for greasing

☆ METHOD ☆

1. Sift the flour, salt and baking powder together into a large bowl, then make a well in the centre. Beat the buttermilk and egg together in a jug, add to the well and gradually beat in the flour mixture from around the sides to make a smooth batter.
2. Heat a large nonstick frying pan over a medium heat. Brush with oil. Drop 3 tablespoonfuls of the batter into the pan to make 3 pancakes. Cook for 2–3 minutes until bubbles start to appear on the surface and the underside is golden brown. Flip over and cook for a further 2 minutes.
3. Meanwhile, place the blueberries, orange juice and vanilla sugar, to taste, in a small saucepan. Warm over a low heat until the blueberries begin to burst.
4. To serve, place a stack of pancakes on to each warmed serving plate and spoon over the warm vanilla blueberries. Add a dollop of crème fraîche if liked (optional).

Take Me Back to the COUNTRY HAM

SERVES 10–12 | PREP: 5mins

COOKING TIME: 2 hours 25 minutes–3 hours

There's nothing like a slice or two of country ham to set you up for the day, especially when eaten with a pile of tasty Tennessee Mountain Home Fries (see page 44). Tip: There's usually no need to soak a ham before cooking these days as they are mostly cured with less salt. If in doubt (or you prefer a less salty flavour), soak a small ham for around 8 hours in cold water, or a larger ham for up to 24 hours.

☆ INGREDIENTS ☆

2.5–4kg (5½–8½lb) gammon joint, either on the bone or boned and rolled

2 bay leaves

8 tablespoons demerara sugar

3 tablespoons ginger marmalade

150ml (¼ pint) ginger ale

☆ METHOD ☆

1. Either follow the pack instructions or calculate the cooking time of the ham based on 25 minutes per 500g (1lb), plus 20 minutes. For a joint over 3kg (6½ lb), allow 20 minutes per 500g (1lb), plus 20 minutes. Place in a large pan and cover with fresh cold water. Add the bay leaves and 2 tablespoons of the sugar and bring to the boil. Cover, reduce the heat and simmer for half the calculated cooking time.
2. Remove the gammon from the water and strip off the skin. Stand the joint on a large sheet of foil in a roasting tin and score the fat diagonally in a trellis pattern. Mix the marmalade and remaining sugar and spread over the fat. Pour the ginger ale around the joint and enclose in the foil, sealing the edges firmly.
3. Bake in a preheated oven, 190°C (375°F), Gas Mark 5, for the remaining cooking time. During cooking, baste the gammon with the ginger ale, then rewrap in the foil. About 20 minutes before the end of the cooking time, fold back the foil, baste again and return to the oven. Leave to cool overnight.

• FUN FACT •

Dolly and her sister, Rachel Parton George, recommended serving country ham as part of their New Year's Day feast in their book, *Good Lookin' Cookin'* which they wrote together in 2024.

9 To 5 Breakfast MUFFINS

SERVES 12 | PREP: 10mins | COOKING TIME: 20–25mins

Make these quick and easy breakfast muffins in the evening and they'll be ready to grab and go when you're stumblin' to the kitchen and hustlin' out the door in the morning! Perfect with a cup of coffee while you're waiting for the tide to turn your way!

9 TO 5 BREAKFAST MUFFINS

☆ INGREDIENTS ☆

6 streaky bacon rashers, excess fat removed, finely chopped

1 small red onion, finely chopped

200g (7oz) sweetcorn

175g (6oz) fine cornmeal

125g (4oz) plain flour

2 teaspoons baking powder

50g (2oz) Cheddar cheese, grated

200ml (7fl oz) skimmed milk

2 eggs

3 tablespoons vegetable oil

☆ METHOD ☆

1. Lightly oil a 12-hole muffin tin.
2. Dry-fry the bacon and onion in a nonstick frying pan over a medium heat for 3–4 minutes until the bacon is turning crisp.
3. Put the cornmeal, flour and baking powder in a bowl and mix. Add the sweetcorn, cheese, bacon and onions, then stir in.
4. Whisk the milk with the eggs and oil in a separate bowl, then add to the dry ingredients. Stir gently until just combined, then divide the mixture between the muffin tin sections.
5. Bake in a preheated oven, 220°C (425°F), Gas Mark 7, for 15–20 minutes until golden and just firm. Loosen the edges of the muffins with a knife and transfer to a wire rack to cool.

• FUN FACT •

Dolly and her siblings would help harvest the corn that grew on their family farm when growing up in the mountains of East Tennessee.

Bluegrass GRANOLA

SERVES 6 | PREP: 20mins, plus cooling

COOKING TIME: 5–8mins

Bluegrass music is characterised by guitars, banjos and close-harmony vocals, combining to create what Dolly calls 'Mountain music'. This combination of granola ingredients offers a perfect harmony of flavours in each and every spoonful! All you need to do is imagine sitting on your porch and watch the sunrise over the Smoky Mountains as you eat them!

BLUEGRASS GRANOLA

☆ INGREDIENTS ☆

FOR THE GRANOLA

2 tablespoons olive oil

2 tablespoons maple syrup

40g (1½ oz) flaked almonds

40g (1½ oz) pine nuts

25g (1oz) sunflower seeds

25g (1oz) porridge oats

375g (12oz) natural yogurt

2 tablespoons pecans, chopped

FOR THE FRUIT SALAD [PER PERSON]

6 strawberries, halved

handful of red seedless grapes, halved

2 slices cantaloupe melon, cubed

grated rind and juice of 1 lime

☆ METHOD ☆

1. Heat the oil in a flameproof frying pan with a metal handle, add the maple syrup and the nuts, seeds and oats and toss together.
2. Transfer the pan to a preheated oven, 180°C (350°F), Gas Mark 4, and cook for 5–8 minutes, stirring once and moving the brown edges to the centre, until the granola mixture is evenly toasted.
3. Leave the mixture to cool, then pack it into a storage jar, seal, label and consume within 10 days.
4. Make the fruit salad. Mix the fruits with the lime rind and juice, spoon the mixture into dishes and top with a tablespoon of natural yogurt and the granola.

Little Bit Country
· BREAKFAST SKILLET ·

SERVES 4 | PREP: 10mins | COOKING TIME: 35mins

This version of a traditional breakfast skillet is cooked in the oven so that you can be getting yourself lookin' just fine without having to tend to a stovetop pan! Leave out the sausages to turn this into a satisfying vegetarian option. Ideal for low-maintenance brunches with your gal pals, served with a Steel Magnolia Spritz (see page 119).

LITTLE BIT COUNTRY BREAKFAST SKILLET

☆ INGREDIENTS ☆

500g (1lb) cooked potatoes, cubed

4 tablespoons olive oil

3–4 thyme sprigs

4 pork sausages, each chopped into 5 chunks

250g (8oz) button mushrooms, trimmed

12 cherry tomatoes

4 eggs

salt and black pepper

2 tablespoons chopped parsley, to garnish

buttered toast, to serve (optional)

☆ METHOD ☆

1. Spread the potato cubes out in a roasting tin. Drizzle over half the oil, scatter over the thyme sprigs and season with salt and pepper. Add the chopped sausages and bake in a preheated oven, 220°C (425°F), Gas Mark 7, for 10 minutes.
2. Stir the potato and sausage mixture well, then add the mushrooms and bake for 10 minutes. Add the tomatoes and bake for a further 10 minutes.
3. Make four hollows in between the vegetables and carefully break an egg into each hollow. Bake for 3–4 minutes until the eggs are set. Garnish with the parsley and serve straight from the tin, with buttered toast.

• FUN FACT •

Dolly loves playing around with her hair and make-up, and has said she must own "at least 365 wigs" because she wears one every day!

Fill Your Working Boots FLAPJACKS

SERVES 4 | PREP: 10mins | COOKING TIME: 22mins

Try to resist eating these flapjacks hot from the tin, as they'll be bubbling over with hot honey goodness! Easy to adapt, why not add raisins or add nuts to the recipe to make an energy-giving fruit and protein breakfast bar?

FILL YOUR WORKING BOOTS FLAPJACKS

★ INGREDIENTS ★

vegetable oil, for greasing

2g (1oz) light muscovado sugar

175g (6oz) unsalted butter

1 tablespoon clear honey

1½ tablespoons golden syrup (corn syrup)

1 large banana, mashed

300g (10oz) rolled oats

75g (3oz) dried banana chips, roughly broken

★ METHOD ★

1. Lightly grease a 22cm (8½ inch) square cake tin.
2. Place the sugar, butter, honey and golden syrup in a saucepan over a medium heat and heat, stirring occasionally, until the butter is melted and the sugar dissolved. Remove from the heat.
3. Stir in the mashed banana and oats and mix well. Spoon one-half of the oat mixture into the prepared tin, sprinkle over the banana chips and top with the remaining oat mixture. Press down and level the top.
4. Bake in a preheated oven, 180°C (350°F), Gas Mark 4, for 20–22 minutes until golden. Remove from the oven and cut into 12 bars while still hot. Leave to cool in the tin.

• FUN FACT •

As a child, Dolly would get up at dawn to chat to her daddy before he went to work and help pack his lunch in a green 'dinner bucket'. 'Daddy's Working Boots' and 'The Dinner Bucket' are songs written by Dolly that share memories of her hard-working father.

Lunch
DOLLY

Backwoods Barbie-Cue CHICKEN

SERVES 4 | PREP: 10mins | COOKING TIME: 20mins

In 2007, Dolly told *The Sun* newspaper, "Maybe I am just a Backwoods Barbie – too much make-up, too much hair, in a push up bra and heels ... It might look artificial but where it counts, I'm real." This barbecue recipe is also the real deal, with big hitting flavours that come from regular ol' store-cupboard ingredients. Use the sauce on chicken, pork, shrimp, vegetable skewers or anything else you like to throw onto the grill!

BACKWOODS BARBIE-CUE CHICKEN

☆ INGREDIENTS ☆

6 tablespoons tomato ketchup

2 tablespoons Worcestershire sauce

2 tablespoons red wine vinegar

2 tablespoons light muscovado sugar

2 teaspoons English mustard

4 chicken breasts

☆ METHOD ☆

1. Mix the ketchup, Worcestershire sauce, vinegar, sugar and mustard together. Put the chicken on a foil-lined baking sheet or grill rack, then brush with the ketchup mixture.

2. Cook the chicken under a preheated grill or on a barbecue for about 20 minutes. Turn once or twice until a deep brown and the chicken is cooked through, with no pink meat remaining. Serve with ketchup and fries or salad.

Tennessee BARBECUE RIBS

SERVES 4 | PREP: 25mins, plus marinating

COOKING TIME: 3hrs 10mins

The smell of these ribs as they slowly cook is going to make your mouth water but just be patient – the wait will be worth it! The dry rub can be stored in an airtight container for up to 1 month. If marinating the ribs in it overnight, allow them to stand at room temperature for 30 minutes before cooking.

• FUN FACT •

Live the country dream by spritzing yourself with Tennessee Sunset – a fragrance by Dolly that combines the scents from around her mountain home including honeysuckle and vanilla orchid!

TENNESSEE BARBECUE RIBS

☆ INGREDIENTS ☆

FOR THE BARBECUE RUB, COMBINE

1 tablespoon salt
1 tablespoon smoked paprika
1 teaspoon ground coriander
2 teaspoons crushed black pepper
2 teaspoons mustard powder
1 teaspoon caster sugar
¼ teaspoon cayenne pepper

FOR THE SPARE RIBS

1kg (2lb) pork spare rib rack
1 tablespoon olive oil, plus extra for brushing
3 tablespoons water

FOR THE BARBECUE SAUCE

250ml (8fl oz) tomato purée
125ml (4fl oz) treacle
75ml (3fl oz) maple syrup
75ml (3fl oz) white wine vinegar
2 tablespoons Worcestershire sauce
1 tablespoon Dijon mustard
1 teaspoon garlic powder
¼ teaspoon smoked paprika
salt and black pepper

☆ METHOD ☆

1. Place the ribs in a non-metallic dish. Mix the barbecue rub with the olive oil and rub all over the ribs. Cover and leave to marinate for 1 hour, or overnight in the refrigerator.
2. Transfer the ribs to a baking tray and pour the water around them. Cover tightly with foil and cook in a preheated oven, 160°C (325°F), Gas Mark 3, for 3 hours.
3. Place all the ingredients for the barbecue sauce in a saucepan and heat gently until boiling. Simmer gently for 10–15 minutes until the sauce has thickened slightly.
4. Brush the sauce over the ribs and return to the oven, uncovered, for 10 minutes. Slice before serving.

Heart Of The Smokies BBQ Wings

SERVES 4 | PREP: 12mins | COOKING TIME: 15–17mins

These mighty and magic hot wings will call you home to the Great Smoky Mountains. Be sure to claim the recipe as your own and show your friends some good old Southern hospitality by making enough to share! After all, Dolly isn't just the queen of country, she's the owner of a hospitality empire. She loves inviting visitors to discover the beauty of her childhood home in Pigeon Forge and has built an amusement park, resort and restaurants there that celebrate its beauty and magic. Let's go!

HEART OF THE SMOKIES BBQ WINGS

☆ INGREDIENTS ☆

FOR THE WINGS

2 tablespoons oil

4 tablespoons tomato ketchup

3 tablespoons sweet chilli sauce

½ teaspoon chilli flakes

1 tablespoon clear honey

½ teaspoons ground black pepper

750g (1½ lb) chicken wings

FOR THE APPLE SLAW

1 dessert apple, cored, diced

1 tablespoon lemon juice

1 carrot, coarsely grated

3 spring onions, thinly sliced

200g (7oz) white cabbage, finely shredded, core discarded

6 tablespoons light mayonnaise

salt and pepper

☆ METHOD ☆

1. Mix together the oil, ketchup, chilli sauce, chilli flakes, honey and pepper in a large mixing bowl, add the chicken wings and stir well to coat each in the mixture.
2. Arrange the wings in a single layer on a foil-lined grill rack and cook under a preheated hot grill for 10 minutes on one side, before turning and cooking for 5–7 minutes on the other until the chicken is cooked through.
3. Meanwhile, mix all the slaw ingredients together in a bowl, then spoon into a serving dish. Put the chicken wings on to a plate and serve immediately.

Here I Goat (Again) CHEESE TART

SERVES 4 | PREP: 10mins

COOKING TIME: 20 mins, plus cooling

The crossover country/pop song that inspired this tangy cheese and tomato tart won Best Country Vocal Performance (Female) in 1979 and reached number 3 in the Billboard Hot 100. Pack yourself a bucket load of willpower to resist eating more than one slice. It's sure to fill up your senses and make you lose your defences!

HERE I GOAT (AGAIN) CHEESE TART

☆ INGREDIENTS ☆

375g (12oz) ready-rolled puff pastry

flour, for dusting

8 tablespoons chilli jam

400g (13oz) mixed red and yellow cherry tomatoes, halved

200g (7oz) soft goats' cheese

4 tablespoons finely chopped mint leaves, to garnish

green salad, to serve (optional)

☆ METHOD ☆

1. Unroll the puff pastry on to a lightly floured work surface and cut into a 30 x 20cm (12 x 8inch) rectangle. Using a sharp knife, score a border 2cm (¾ inch) from the edge of the pastry. Put the pastry on a baking sheet and place in a preheated oven, 220°C (425°F), Gas Mark 7, for 10–12 minutes or until the pastry has risen and is cooked through and lightly golden. Cool for 5 minutes.
2. Spoon the chilli jam evenly over the base of the puff pastry case, then top with the tomatoes. Crumble over the goats' cheese and return the filled tart to the oven for 6–8 minutes or until the cheese has melted and the tart has heated through.
3. Scatter over the chopped mint and serve with a green salad (optional).

• FUN FACT •

'Here You Come Again' was written by Barry Mann and Cynthia Weil, who also scored huge hits with the Righteous Brothers and the Drifters.

Hillbilly Halloumi FAJITAS

SERVES 4 | PREP: 15mins | COOKING TIME: 20mins

Dolly's music has been described as cheesy and corny ... well, if those food metaphors are good enough for Dolly, they're good enough for us! These fajitas make a delicious meat-free summer lunch, but you can substitute in any protein (and serve with corncobs on the side). If the mixture seems a little dry during cooking, stir in a tablespoon of water and sizzle up a storm!

DOLLY SAYS

"I'm proud of my hillbilly, white trash background. To me that keeps you humble; that keeps you good."

HILLBILLY HALLOUMI FAJITAS

☆ INGREDIENTS ☆

FOR THE FAJITAS

2 tablespoons olive oil

1 red, 1 green and 1 orange pepper, thinly sliced

400g (13oz) halloumi cheese

2 red onions, cut into thin wedges

1 tablespoon Cajun spice mix

2 teaspoons lime juice

8 soft flour tortilla wraps, warmed

soured cream, to serve

tortilla chips, to serve (optional)

salsa, to serve (optional)

FOR THE GUACAMOLE

1 avocado, peeled, stoned and roughly chopped

finely grated zest and juice of ½ lime

salt and pepper

☆ METHOD ☆

1. Cut the halloumi into slices of around 7–8mm (¼–½ inch) and then in half lengthwise to make long fingers of cheese. Heat 1 tablespoon of the oil in a heavy-based frying pan and cook over a medium heat for 2–3 minutes on each side until golden.
2. Add the rest of the oil to the pan and cook the peppers and onions over a high heat for 5 minutes until lightly charred in places. Return the halloumi to the pan and add the Cajun spice and lime juice. Toss and stir-fry for a further 10 minutes until the vegetables are softened.
3. Make the guacamole. Put the avocado in a bowl and mash well with a fork until smooth but still textured. Season with salt and pepper, add the lime zest and juice and stir to combine.
4. Fill the warmed tortillas with the fajita mixture, soured cream and guacamole. Serve with tortilla chips and salsa (optional).

CHICKEN DIPPERS
Every Sunday

SERVES 4 | PREP: 20mins | COOKING TIME: 6–8mins

Pay no attention to the ladies social set or the folks at the country club, if you've got chicken dippers every Sunday you're just as good as them! Spice up the salsa by adding some chopped red chilli or red pepper flakes or add a warming kick to the chicken seasoning by including a teaspoon of paprika.

☆ INGREDIENTS ☆

FOR THE SALSA

2 tomatoes, diced

¼ cucumber, diced

75g (3oz) sweetcorn

1 tablespoon fresh coriander leaves, chopped

FOR THE CHICKEN DIPPERS

2 eggs

2 tablespoons milk

100g (3½ oz) fresh breadcrumbs

4 tablespoons freshly grated Parmesan cheese

500g (1lb) boneless, skinless chicken breasts

25g (1oz) butter

2 tablespoons vegetable oil

salt and pepper

☆ METHOD ☆

1. Put the salsa ingredients in a bowl and mix together.
2. Beat the eggs, milk and a little salt and pepper together in a dish.
3. Mix the breadcrumbs with the Parmesan in a shallow dish.
4. Dip one chicken strip into the egg mixture, then roll in the breadcrumbs. Carry on doing this until all the chicken strips are well covered.
5. Heat the butter and oil in a large frying pan and add the chicken strips. Cook for 6–8 minutes, turning a few times until they are brown all over. Serve with the salsa.

• FUN FACT •

'Chicken Every Sunday' comes from Dolly's 1971 album, *Joshua*, which was one of three solo albums she released that year!

In The Garden SALAD

SERVES 4 | PREP: 10mins

A garden salad can use any combination of greens and vegetables, so include whatever is fresh and seasonal to this base bowl of crunchy goodness. This combination of flavours work in perfect harmony, much like the Parton family, who used to sing together over the stove when Dolly was a girl. In fact, four of them recorded an album called *The Parton Family Sings "In the Garden"* in 1968, a year after Dolly's first album was released!

☆ INGREDIENTS ☆

FOR THE SALAD

½ cucumber

250g (8oz) cherry tomatoes

250g (8oz) baby leaf mix

1 avocado

50g (2oz) pitted black olives

FOR THE DRESSING

1 teaspoon Dijon mustard

2 tablespoons cider vinegar

3 tablespoons olive oil

salt and pepper

☆ METHOD ☆

1. Peel and slice the cucumber and halve the tomatoes. Mix the salad leaves with the cucumber and tomatoes in a large salad bowl. Stone and peel the avocado, cut the flesh into dice and add to the bowl with the olives.
2. Make the dressing by whisking together the mustard, vinegar and oil. Season to taste with salt and pepper.
3. Pour the dressing over the salad, toss carefully to combine and serve.

Sawmill Biscuits & Gravy

SERVES 4 | PREP: 20mins | COOKING TIME: 15–20mins

This southern breakfast recipe, traditionally eaten by lumberjacks working in sawmills, makes a filling brunch. Use English breakfast muffins, ready-made biscuits or bake them yourself for a taste of Southern Appalachia. Dolly has often described how the sounds of her home influenced her songwriting, telling ABC News in 2019, "Everything was music to me ... if someone was hammering on the other hill at the sawmill, I'd start writing a song with that rhythm." This dish is a tribute to those inspirational workers!

SAWMILL BISCUITS & GRAVY

☆ INGREDIENTS ☆

FOR THE BISCUITS

500g (1lb) self-raising flour, plus 1 tablespoon extra for rolling

250g (8oz) butter, chilled

250ml (8fl oz) buttermilk

1 tablespoon butter, melted

FOR THE GRAVY

400g (13oz) pork sausages, chopped

25g (1oz) flour

600ml (1 pint) whole milk

1 teaspoon garlic powder

½ teaspoon onion powder

½ teaspoon dried thyme

½ teaspoon paprika

salt and pepper

¼ teaspoon red chilli flakes

☆ METHOD ☆

1. Put the flour in a large bowl. Grate in the chilled butter and combine to form coarse breadcrumbs. Pour in the buttermilk. Mix with a spatula until a soft, sticky dough forms, then knead for 1 minute.
2. Pat or roll the dough into a flat rectangle, fold it in half, then roll out again. Repeat the folding and rolling twice more, ending with a rectangle approx. 2.5cm (1inch) thick. Cut out the biscuits using a 7cm (3inch) cutter. Bake on a lined baking sheet in a preheated oven, 230°C (450°F), Gas Mark 8, for 12–14 minutes or until risen and golden. Remove from the oven and brush with the melted butter.
3. Make the gravy by briskly frying the chopped sausage over a medium-high heat. Break the sausage down until it is brown and crumbly. Sprinkle over the flour and cook for 1 minute. Add the remaining dry ingredients then gradually pour in the milk. Stir as the gravy thickens, around 6–7 minutes. Simmer for 5 minutes, stirring frequently. Season to taste and serve spooned over the warm biscuits.

I Don't Want To Throw RISOTTO

SERVES 4 | PREP: 10mins | COOKING TIME 30mins

Much like some relationships, taking things slow and steady is the key to a perfect risotto. So, stir, stir, and stir again to stop the risotto from sticking and you'll avoid the kind of heartbreak that the lyrics of 'I Don't Want to Throw Rice' describe!

• FUN FACT •

Dolly met her husband, Carl Dean, on the day she arrived in Nashville, Tennessee. Carl later said, "My first thought was I'm gonna marry that girl." They remained happily married until his death in 2025.

☆ INGREDIENTS ☆

50g (2oz) butter

2 shallots, finely chopped

1 mild red chilli, thinly sliced

1 teaspoon mild paprika

1 garlic clove, crushed

300g (10oz) risotto rice

150ml (¼ pint) dry white wine

2–3 lemon thyme sprigs

approx. 1.2 litres (2 pints) hot fish stock or chicken stock

3 tablespoons chopped tarragon

300g (10oz) cooked crayfish tails in brine, drained

Parmesan cheese, to garnish

☆ METHOD ☆

1. Melt half the butter in a large saucepan or deep-sided sauté pan and gently fry the shallots until softened. Add the chilli, paprika and garlic and continue to fry for 30 seconds, without browning the garlic.
2. Sprinkle in the rice and fry gently for 1 minute, stirring. Add the wine and let it bubble until almost evaporated.
3. Add the thyme and a ladleful of the stock and cook, stirring regularly, until the rice has almost absorbed the stock. Continue cooking, adding the stock a ladleful at a time, and letting the rice absorb most of the stock before adding more. Once the rice is tender but retaining a little bite, the risotto is ready – around 25 minutes. You may not need all the stock.
4. Stir in the tarragon, crayfish and remaining butter and heat through gently for 1 minute. Serve immediately with grated Parmesan.

My Tennessee Mountain HOME FRIES

SERVES 4 | PREP: 5mins | COOKING TIME: 30-35mins

Home fries are a breakfast staple in the Southern states of the US of A but they taste just dandy at any time of the day! This version suggests parboiling the potatoes first for speed, but you can also toss them straight into the skillet to cook. Serve with whatever you fancy, or with the country ham from page 14.

MY TENNESSEE MOUNTAIN HOME FRIES

☆ INGREDIENTS ☆

500g (1lb) floury white potatoes, peeled and cut into cubes

2 tablespoons vegetable oil

1 onion, finely chopped

2 teaspoons ground paprika

salt and pepper

3 tablespoons chopped parsley

☆ METHOD ☆

1. Bring a large saucepan of lightly salted water to the boil and cook the potatoes for 10 minutes. Drain.
2. Heat the oil in a large, heavy-based frying pan and fry the onions over a medium heat until softened, around 5 minutes. Add the potatoes and stir well to coat the potatoes in the oil over a high heat for 5 minutes until golden.
3. Lower the heat to a medium heat and sprinkle over the paprika. Cook until golden on all sides, stirring at least once, for around 10 more minutes. Season with salt and pepper and toss in the parsley before serving.

• FUN FACT •

Dolly's 1972 song, 'My Tennessee Mountain Home' was named an official state song in 2022!

Hall Of Fame
· MAC AND CHEESE ·

SERVES 4 | PREP: 15mins | COOKING TIME: 35–40mins

There's nothing more satisfying than a big bowl of mac and cheese – and Dolly would certainly agree. As a huge fan of this classic comfort food, Dolly's own recipe is such a hit, she even sells a ready-made version! This version is also a crowd-pleaser, so fill your boots!

HALL OF FAME MAC AND CHEESE

☆ INGREDIENTS ☆

200g (7oz) macaroni

40g (1½ oz) butter

40g (1½ oz) plain flour

500ml (17fl oz) milk

1 teaspoon Dijon mustard

100g (5oz) Cheddar cheese, coarsely grated

50g (2oz) mozzarella cheese, coarsely grated

65g (2½ oz) panko breadcrumbs

☆ METHOD ☆

1. Cook the macaroni for about 10 minutes or according to packet instructions until al dente. Drain and put on one side.
2. Melt 40g (1½ oz) of the butter in the rinsed and dried saucepan. Add the flour and stir it in with a wooden spoon. Cook over a gentle heat, stirring, for 1 minute. Remove the pan from the heat and gradually pour in the milk, whisking well. Return the pan to the heat and cook over a gentle heat, stirring continuously until the sauce is thickened and smooth, around 5–6 minutes.
3. Add the mustard, Cheddar and mozzarella and stir until the cheeses have melted. Tip in the macaroni and stir to coat the pasta in the sauce, then pour into a shallow heatproof dish.
4. Sprinkle the panko breadcrumbs over the macaroni and cook in a preheated oven, 180°C (350°F), Gas Mark 4, for 25 minutes.

• FUN FACT •

Dolly was inducted into the Country Music Hall of Fame in 1999, but declined a nomination for the Rock and Roll Hall of Fame in 2022, saying she hoped they would consider her again "if I'm ever worthy".

Wrapped Up In You Shrimps

SERVES 4 | PREP 10mins

It's time for a Jolly Dolly Holiday, guys and gals! If ever you feel blue during the most wonderful time of the year, this lightweight lunch will help ease the pressure on your waistband and your time. It's so quick to prepare you'll be back to gift wrapping before you know it!

WRAPPED UP IN YOU SHRIMPS

☆ INGREDIENTS ☆

2 tablespoons low-fat crème fraîche

2 teaspoons tomato ketchup

few drops of Tabasco sauce, to taste

300g (10oz) cooked peeled shrimps

1 mango, peeled, stoned and thinly sliced

1 avocado, peeled, stoned and sliced

4 flour tortillas

100g (3½ oz) watercress

☆ METHOD ☆

1. Mix together the crème fraîche, ketchup and Tabasco to taste in a bowl.
2. Add the prawns, mango and avocado and toss the mixture together.
3. Spoon the mixture into the tortillas, add some sprigs of watercress, roll up and serve.

• FUN FACT •

Dolly has released three Christmas albums, and 2020's *A Holly Dolly Christmas* included duets with Michael Bublé, Miley Cyrus and country legend, Willie Nelson.

Please Don't Stop Loving MISO AUBERGINES

SERVES 4 | PREP: 10mins | COOKING TIME: 20mins

Miso is a paste used in Asian cuisine made from soybeans, and has a savoury, umami flavour which is especially popular in Japanese food. If you can't find miso, soy sauce will add a similar depth and saltiness to the grilled aubergine. The richness of this part of the dish is tempered by the coolness of the salad, making this a meal you'll never stop loving!

PLEASE DON'T STOP LOVING MISO AUBERGINES

☆ INGREDIENTS ☆

12 baby aubergines, halved
4 tablespoons white miso paste
3 tablespoons rice wine vinegar
2 tablespoons caster sugar
1 tablespoon saké or water
1 tablespoon sesame seeds
125g (4oz) soya beans
300g (10oz) ready-cooked rice noodles
½ cucumber, thinly sliced
2 spring onions, thinly sliced
salt

☆ METHOD ☆

1. Make a criss-cross pattern on the cut sides of the aubergines and place them, cut side down, on a grill pan. Cook for 7–10 minutes under a preheated hot grill until charred.
2. Mix the miso paste, 2 tablespoons vinegar, the sugar and saké or water. Turn the aubergines over and brush with the miso mixture. Return to the grill for 3–5 minutes until the aubergine is soft, then sprinkle with the sesame seeds and cook for 1 minute more.
3. Meanwhile, cook the soya beans in a saucepan of lightly salted boiling water for 2 minutes until soft. Drain and cool under cold running water.
4. Toss the beans together with the noodles, cucumber, spring onions, the remaining vinegar and season with salt. Serve with the grilled aubergine.

• FUN FACT •

'Please Don't Stop Loving Me' was sung by Dolly and her country co-star, Porter Wagoner. Dolly performed on Porter's musical variety TV show for seven years early in her career.

Dinner

Dollywood DUMPLINGS

SERVES 4 | PREP: 25mins | COOKING TIME: 1½ hours

Dollywood opened in Pigeon Forge, Tennessee in 1986 and every year, some 3 million guests flock to this theme park and resort, close to the Great Smoky Mountains. Build yourself some stamina ahead of your own visit to this 165-acre site by indulging in this hearty chicken and dumpling dinner!

• FUN FACT •

A replica of the cabin Dolly grew up in was built inside the park by her brother, Bobby!

DOLLYWOOD DUMPLINGS

☆ INGREDIENTS ☆

3 tablespoons olive oil

8 skinned and boned chicken thighs, diced

4 teaspoons Cajun spice

1 large onion, sliced

100g (3½ oz) smoked streaky bacon, chopped

2 red and 2 yellow peppers, roughly chopped

200ml (7fl oz) chicken stock (see page 16)

125g (4oz) self-raising flour

125g (4oz) cornmeal

½ teaspoon dried chilli flakes

3 tablespoons chopped fresh coriander

75g (3oz) Cheddar cheese, grated

50g (2oz) butter, melted

1 egg

100ml (3½ fl oz) milk

4 small tomatoes, skinned and quartered

100ml (3½ fl oz) double cream

salt and pepper

ADMIT ONE

☆ METHOD ☆

1. Heat the oil in a large, shallow flameproof casserole dish and fry the chicken pieces for about 5 minutes until lightly browned. Stir in the spice blend and cook for a further 1 minute. Drain to a plate. Fry the onion, bacon and peppers for 10 minutes, stirring frequently.

2. Return the chicken to the dish. Stir in the stock and a little seasoning. Bring to the boil, then cover and bake in a preheated oven, 180°C (350°F), Gas Mark 4, for 45 minutes.

3. Make the dumplings: mix the flour, cornmeal, chilli flakes, coriander and cheese in a bowl. Beat the butter with the egg and milk and add to make a thick paste. It should be fairly sticky but hold its shape.

4. Stir the tomatoes and cream into the chicken mixture, season to taste. Place spoons of the dumpling mixture over the top. Return to the oven, uncovered, for a further 30 minutes or until the dumplings have slightly risen and form a firm crust.

Just When I Needed You ROAST

SERVES 4 | PREP: 15mins | COOKING TIME: 30mins

You'll be in hog heaven with this spicy-seasoned pork, served here over mustardy vegetables. The beauty of this dish is its flexibility – the vegetables go well with any meat, and the pork can form part of a traditional roast dinner or be eaten with stir-fried rice or a bulgar salad. Let it putter away on the stove while you write a letter to the person you need the most …

JUST WHEN I NEEDED YOU ROAST

☆ INGREDIENTS ☆

FOR THE RUB

1 teaspoon ground cumin

1 teaspoon ground coriander

FOR THE PORK AND VEGETABLES

3 tablespoons olive oil

500g (1lb) pork loin, trimmed of fat

300g (10oz) sweet potatoes, peeled and chopped

250g (8oz) savoy cabbage, shredded

3 leeks, trimmed and sliced

3 tablespoons soured cream

2 teaspoons wholegrain mustard

☆ METHOD ☆

1. Mix the rub spices in a bowl, then rub over the pork. Heat 1 tablespoon of the olive oil in an ovenproof frying pan, add the pork and cook until browned on all sides. Transfer to a preheated oven, 180°C (350°F), Gas Mark 4, and cook for 20–25 minutes or until cooked through. Leave to rest for 2 minutes.
2. Meanwhile, cook the sweet potatoes in a saucepan of boiling water for 12–15 minutes until tender, adding the cabbage and leeks 3–4 minutes before the end of the cooking time. Drain well.
3. Heat the remaining oil in a frying pan, add the cooked vegetables and fry for 7–8 minutes until starting to turn golden. Stir in the cream and mustard.
4. Slice the pork and serve on top of the vegetables.

I Will Always Love FONDUE

SERVES 4 | PREP: 10mins | COOKING TIME: 30mins

'I Will Always Love You' was written by Dolly in 1973, but it was Whitney Houston's cover from the 1992 movie, *The Bodyguard*, that made this song a global phenomenon. When she first heard Houston's version, Dolly said, "That was one of the greatest experiences I've ever had in my entire life." Now it's your turn to impress your guests with this classic fondue recipe which will hit all the right notes.

I WILL ALWAYS LOVE FONDUE

✯ INGREDIENTS ✯

TO SERVE

selection of dippers, such as cubes of crusty bread or vegetable sticks

FOR THE FONDUE

1 garlic clove, peeled and halved

200ml (7fl oz) dry white wine or cider + 2 tablespoons

1½ tablespoons cornflour

500g (1lb) mixture of grated cheese (such as Emmental, Gruyère and Cheddar)

100ml (3½ fl oz) double cream

✯ METHOD ✯

1. Rub the cut side of the garlic all over the inside of a saucepan, then discard. Pour 250ml (8fl oz) dry white wine or cider into the pan and bring to the boil.
2. Stir 1 tablespoon cornflour into the 2 reserved tablespoons of wine or cider, then pour into the simmering pan in a slow, steady drizzle, stirring constantly until thickened.
3. Add the cheese and double cream and stir frequently over a low heat until melted.
4. Transfer the saucepan directly to the table, placing it on a heatproof mat or board or scrape the cheese into a warmed fondue dish with a tealight below, following the manufacturer's instructions for heating. Serve with a selection of dippers.

Jolene's TAGINE

SERVES 4 | PREP: 15mins

COOKING TIME: 45mins, plus 10mins finishing

A tagine is a North African spiced stew, slow-cooked in an earthenware dish with a tall, conical lid. (It's also the name of the dish used for cooking the tagine.) However, there's no need for any specialist cookware to make this all-in-one-pan Jolene Tagine – whatever you decide to do, it will bubble along nicely in a large saucepan or shallow casserole dish. Give it a go, just because you can!

JOLENE'S TAGINE

★ INGREDIENTS ★

2 tablespoons sunflower oil

2 onions, roughly chopped

1 teaspoon smoked paprika

1 teaspoon ground turmeric

2 teaspoons cumin seeds, roughly crushed

500g (1lb) potatoes, scrubbed and cubed

400g (13oz) can chickpeas, drained

40g (13oz) can pinto beans, drained

100g (3½ oz) pickled lemons, drained and quartered

600ml (1 pint) vegetable stock

salt and pepper

small bunch of coriander, to serve

125g (4oz) feta cheese, crumbled (optional)

★ METHOD ★

1. Heat the oil in a saucepan or shallow casserole dish, add the onion and fry for 5 minutes until lightly browned. Stir in the spices and cook for 1 minute. Mix in the potatoes and drained pulses and stir well.
2. Add the pickled lemons, stock and seasoning. Bring to the boil then reduce the heat, cover and simmer gently for 40 minutes until the potatoes are tender.
3. Spoon into shallow bowls and top with torn coriander leaves and feta cheese, if using.

Working 9 To 5 SPICE DUCK

SERVES 4 | PREP: 10mins | COOKING TIME: 30mins

When writing the theme song to the film *9 to 5* (1980), Dolly took inspiration from the sound her acrylic nails made when rubbed together – their sharp clicking reminded her of typewriter keys tapping. 'Nails by Dolly' is even given on the song credits for this smash hit! Now it's your turn to take credit for producing this comforting noodle dish which will restore your spirits after a long day working at the coalface!

WORKING 9 TO 5 SPICE DUCK

☆ INGREDIENTS ☆

1 teaspoon Chinese 5-spice powder

1 tablespoon clear honey

2 tablespoons sweet soy sauce

2 large duck breasts, about 450g (1lb) each, skin removed

1 litre (1¾ pints) clear chicken stock

1 garlic clove, thinly sliced

1 tablespoon finely chopped fresh root ginger

2 spring onions, sliced diagonally

150g (5oz) drained bamboo shoots

200g (7oz) bean sprouts

350g (11½ oz) ramen noodles or medium egg noodles

2 teaspoons toasted sesame seeds, to serve

☆ METHOD ☆

1. Mix the Chinese 5-spice powder, honey and 1 tablespoon of the soy sauce together. Score the duck breasts with a sharp knife. Rub the spice mixture all over the score marks and set aside for 5 minutes.
2. Place the duck breasts, scored and spiced-side down, into a heated frying pan and cook for 5–7 minutes until golden. Turn over, and cook for a further 2–3 minutes, then transfer to a small roasting tin and put in a preheated oven, 220°C (425°F), Gas Mark 7 for 5–10 minutes until cooked through. Allow the duck to rest for 2–3 minutes then slice thinly.
3. Meanwhile, put the stock, remaining soy sauce, garlic and ginger in a saucepan over a medium heat and bring to a gentle boil. Simmer for 10 minutes, then add the spring onions and bamboo shoots. Simmer for a further 2 minutes, then stir in the bean sprouts.
4. Cook the noodles in boiling water for 2–3 minutes. Drain. Ladle the soup into deep bowls. Divide the noodles between the bowls, then arrange the sliced duck on top. Sprinkle with sesame seeds and serve.

He's Driving Me JALFREZI

SERVES 4 | PREP: 10mins | COOKING TIME: 20–25mins

Why'd you come in here cookin' like that? Serve this easy-to-make curry with rice and homemade naan (see recipe on page 67) for a dish that'll blow any cowboy or cowgirl's mind! Top tip: The paneer cheese in this spicy curry can easily be excluded to leave you with a delicious vegan dish. Serve with a long, cool glass of White Limozeen Lemonade (see page 117) if it's too hot for y'all!

☆ INGREDIENTS ☆

1 tablespoon vegetable oil

2 red onions, chopped

175g (6oz) jalfrezi curry paste

1 red pepper, chopped

1 green pepper, chopped

1 small head of cauliflower florets

500g (1lb) white potatoes, cubed

1 can chopped tomatoes (approx. 400g (13oz))

200ml (7fl oz) water

250g (8oz) paneer cheese, cubed

2 tablespoons fresh coriander, chopped

rice, to serve

naan, to serve

☆ METHOD ☆

1. Heat the oil in a large saucepan, add the onion and fry for 5 minutes or until translucent. Stir in the curry paste and fry for 1 minute more.
2. Add the peppers, cauliflower and potato and fry for 2–3 minutes, stirring occasionally, then add the tomatoes and water. Stir well and bring to the boil, then lower the heat and simmer for 12–15 minutes or until all the vegetables are cooked. If the curry starts to stick to the base of the pan, add more water.
3. Add the paneer and simmer for 5 minutes or until it has warmed through. Stir in the coriander and serve with rice and naan.

• FUN FACT •

'Why'd You Come in Here Lookin' Like That' was Dolly's 16th number one single and comes from the *White Limozeen* album released in 1989.

Please Don't Take My NAAN

MAKES 8 | **PREP:** 20 mins, plus resting

COOKING TIME: up to 20mins

In 2022, Dolly debunked the urban myth that she wrote 'Jolene' and 'I Will Always Love You' on the same day in 1973. Apparently, both songs were originally recorded on the same cassette tape but could have been written a few days apart. They appeared on the same album, *Jolene*, in 1974, but the story of this impressive creative feat lives on! This naan makes the perfect accompaniment to the jalfrezi on page 65 – we're beggin' you to make it!

PLEASE DON'T TAKE MY NAAN

☆ INGREDIENTS ☆

450g (14½ oz) self-raising flour

2 teaspoons sugar

1 teaspoon salt

1 teaspoon baking powder

4 tablespoons melted butter or ghee, plus extra for brushing

250ml (8fl oz) warm milk

2 tablespoons nigella seeds

☆ METHOD ☆

1. Sift the flour, sugar, salt and baking powder in a large mixing bowl. Add the melted butter or ghee and rub into the flour mixture with your fingers. Gradually add the warm milk and mix to a soft dough.
2. Transfer to a lightly floured surface and knead for 6–8 minutes or until smooth. Place in the bowl, cover with clingfilm and set aside for 20–25 minutes.
3. Divide the mixture into 8 portions and flatten each one into a thick cake. Cover with a cloth and set aside for 10–15 minutes.
4. Roll each piece into a disc about 23cm (9 inches) in diameter. Brush the tops of the breads with butter or ghee and sprinkle over the nigella seeds.
5. Place the breads on a lightly oiled grill rack and cook in batches under a preheated medium-high grill for 1–2 minutes on each side, or until puffed up and lightly browned in spots. Wrap in a clean tea towel while you finish cooking the rest.

Wrecking MEATBALLS

SERVES 4 | PREP: 25mins | COOKING TIME: 30mins

It's all too easy to fall under the spell of this meatball recipe, and you won't be able to walk away from making them time and time again! Stop at Step 4 if you prefer the meatballs without cheese on top. Serve with pasta or crusty bread for a dinner no one will want to deny!

• FUN FACT •

Miley Cyrus is not only Dolly's goddaughter, she's also her seventh cousin once removed! The singing superstars recorded Miley's smash hit, 'Wrecking Ball', as a duet for Dolly's 2023 *Rockstar* album.

WRECKING MEATBALLS

- 500g (1lb) lean minced beef
- 3 garlic cloves, crushed
- 1 large onion, chopped
- 25g (1oz) breadcrumbs
- 40g (1½ oz) Parmesan cheese
- 6 tablespoons olive oil
- 100ml (3½ fl oz) red wine
- 2 x 400g (13oz) cans chopped tomatoes
- 1 teaspoon caster sugar
- 3 tablespoons sun-dried tomato paste
- 75g (3oz) pitted black olives, chopped
- 4 tablespoons oregano, chopped
- 125g (4oz) mozzarella cheese, thinly sliced
- salt and pepper

METHOD

1. Mix the beef in a bowl with half the crushed garlic, half the onion, the breadcrumbs and 25g (1oz) of the Parmesan. Season, then shape into small balls, about 2.5cm (1 inch) in diameter.
2. Heat half the oil in a large frying pan and fry the meatballs, shaking the pan frequently, for about 10 minutes until browned. Drain and set aside.
3. Add the remaining oil and onion to the pan. Fry until softened. Add the wine and bubble until the wine has almost evaporated. Stir in the remaining garlic, the tomatoes, sugar, tomato paste and a little seasoning. Bring to the boil and bubble until slightly thickened.
4. Stir in the olives, all but 1 tablespoon of the oregano and the meatballs. Cook gently for a further 5 minutes.
5. Arrange the mozzarella slices over the top and scatter with the remaining oregano and Parmesan. Season with black pepper and cook under the grill until the cheese starts to melt. Serve immediately.

Working Lime To Chive CRABCAKES

SERVES 4 | PREP: 15mins, plus chilling

COOKING TIME: 15–18mins

These crabcakes are so quick to prepare, this winner of a dinner will be on the table quicker than you can say 'stage door'! Winner of the People's Choice Award for Best Song in a Movie (1980) and the title of a hit musical written by Dolly herself, *9 to 5*'s plotline about sexism in the workplace still resonates today – as well as having the best theme tune ever!

WORKING LIME TO CHIVE CRABCAKES

☆ INGREDIENTS ☆

2 x 175g (6oz) cans crab meat
3 spring onions, chopped
100g (3½ oz) cooked rice
75g (3oz) dried breadcrumbs
1 red chilli, chopped
3 tablespoons coriander, chopped
2 tablespoons chives, chopped
finely grated zest of ½ lime
1 teaspoon lime juice
2 eggs, lightly beaten
1 teaspoon Thai fish sauce
vegetable oil, for shallow frying
lime wedges, to serve
sweet chilli dipping sauce, to serve

☆ METHOD ☆

1. In a large bowl, mix the crab meat, spring onions, rice, breadcrumbs, chilli, coriander, chives and half of the lime zest. Add the beaten egg and fish sauce to the bowl and mix to combine. Add extra breadcrumbs if the mixture seems a little damp.
2. Form the mixture into 12 crab cakes, place them on a plate, cover lightly and chill in the refrigerator for 10–12 minutes to firm up.
3. Heat the vegetable oil in a large nonstick frying pan and cook the crab cakes for 2–3 minutes on each side, until hot and golden. Drain on kitchen paper and serve with lime wedges and the dipping sauce.

• FUN FACT •

Dolly's sister, Rachel Parton George, appeared in 85 episodes of the TV show, *9 to 5*, playing the same character that her sister made famous in the movie!

What A Way To MAKE A CHICKEN

SERVES 4 | PREP: 10–15mins, plus marinating

COOKING TIME: 10–15mins

It won't be all taking and no giving when you rustle up this flavoursome pasta dish! If you prefer fresh tarragon, use 4 tablespoons, finely chopped. The quantities here make enough to share with family, friends or devoted colleagues!

☆ INGREDIENTS ☆

3 boneless, skinless chicken breasts, cut into thin strips

1 garlic clove, finely chopped

finely grated zest and juice of 1 unwaxed lemon

1 tablespoon olive oil

125g (4oz) broad beans, skinned

250ml (8fl oz) crème fraîche

2 tablespoons tarragon, roughly chopped

400g (13oz) dried tagliatelle

salt and black pepper

☆ METHOD ☆

1. In a non-metallic bowl, coat the chicken strips in the garlic and half the lemon zest and juice. Cover and leave to marinate for 15 minutes.
2. Heat the oil in a large frying pan over a high heat. Season the chicken and add to the pan. Stir for 2 minutes. Stir in the broad beans and fry for a further 1–2 minutes until the chicken is golden and cooked through. Stir in the crème fraîche, tarragon and remaining lemon zest and juice. Season and remove from the heat once the sauce reaches boiling point.
3. Cook the pasta in a large saucepan of salted boiling water until al dente. Drain thoroughly, reserving a ladleful of the cooking water.
4. Tip the pasta into the sauce and toss over a low heat until well combined. If the sauce looks too dry, add a little of the reserved pasta cooking water to give it a silky consistency.

• FUN FACT •

The three leading roles in the movie *9 to 5* were written specifically for Jane Fonda, Lily Tomlin and Dolly – who memorized every line of the script!

Get Your Friends Together PLATTER

MAKES 3–4 JARS | PREP: 10mins

COOKING TIME: 50MINS

With old friends around you, anything is possible, as Dolly and her longtime pals know all too well. Share a spoonful of love with your nearest and dearest by making the homemade chutney that accompanies this charcuterie platter. Recommendations for the basic elements are given here, but can be easily tailored to suit all tastes or dietary preferences.

• FUN FACT •

In the last few years, Dolly has worked with contemporary artists including Sabrina Carpenter, Bebe Rexha and Sia.

GET YOUR FRIENDS TOGETHER PLATTER

☆ INGREDIENTS ☆

FOR THE PLATTER

250–400g (8-13oz) of 5 or 6 of your favourite cheeses, cut into slices or cubes

7–8 slices of your favourite cold meats, quartered and rolled or folded

country ham (see page 15)

chicken dippers (see page 37)

antipasti such as olives and roasted peppers

grapes, to serve

assorted crackers, to serve

FOR THE CHUTNEY

12 peaches

500g (1lb) onions, finely chopped

2 garlic cloves, crushed

2 tablespoons grated root ginger

125g (4oz) pitted dates, chopped

250g (8oz) demerara sugar

300ml (½ pint) red wine vinegar

salt and pepper

☆ METHOD ☆

1. Place the peaches in a large bowl, cover with boiling water and leave to stand for about 1 minute, then drain and peel. Halve and stone the fruit and cut into thick slices.
2. Add the onions to a pan with the peaches, garlic, ginger, dates, sugar and vinegar. Season well and bring to the boil, stirring continuously, until the sugar has completely dissolved.
3. Reduce the heat and simmer the chutney, covered, stirring frequently, for 45 minutes, until thickened.
4. Ladle into warm, dry jars. Disperse any air pockets with a skewer or small knife and cover with screw-top lids. Label and leave to mature in a cool, dark place for at least 3 weeks. Serve with the charcuterie platter.

Hit Me With Your BEST POT PIE

SERVES 4 | PREP: 20mins | COOKING TIME: 45–50mins

Let's get down to it, there's nothing better than the smell of a homecooked pie to soothe the soul after a tough day. And once you've eaten this chicken and vegetable combo, you'll be right back on your feet again. The filling will keep in the refrigerator for two days or in the freezer for up to two months until you're ready to bake it. Defrost thoroughly before proceeding from Step 3 and fire away!

HIT ME WITH YOUR BEST POT PIE

☆ INGREDIENTS ☆

250g (8oz) broccoli florets

1 tablespoon olive oil

375g (12oz) boneless, skinless chicken breasts, cubed

6 streaky bacon rashers, chopped

2 small carrots, chopped

25g (1oz) butter

25g (1oz) plain flour

300ml (½ pint) milk

1 tablespoon white wine vinegar

1 teaspoon Dijon mustard

200ml (7fl oz) crème fraîche

2 tablespoons tarragon or parsley, chopped

500g (1lb) packet shortcrust pastry

beaten egg, for glazing

☆ METHOD ☆

1. Cook the broccoli for 5 minutes until tender. Drain and refresh with cold water, then set aside. Heat the oil in a nonstick frying pan and cook the chicken and bacon over a moderate heat for 7–8 minutes. Add the carrots. Cook for a further 3–4 minutes until golden all over. Remove from the heat.
2. Heat the butter in a medium saucepan and add the flour. Cook over a gentle heat for a few seconds, then remove from the heat and gradually add the milk until well mixed. Add the vinegar and mustard and mix well. Return to the heat and stir continuously until boiled and thickened. Add the crème fraîche and herbs. Tip in the chicken and vegetables and stir well to coat, then transfer to a round pie dish.
3. Roll out the pastry on a floured surface to just larger than the dish. Moisten the rim of the dish lightly with a little water, then place the pastry over the top, trim the edges and decorate with any remaining pastry trimmings if liked. Glaze lightly with the beaten egg. Bake in a preheated oven, 180°C (350°F), Gas Mark 4, for 25–30 minutes until crisp and golden.

For COD & COUNTRY

SERVES 4 | PREP: 5mins | COOKING TIME: 15mins

This dish takes just 20 minutes to make and bake, leaving you time to sit down with a good book of an evening. Dolly is known to millions of children as 'The Book Lady' after she launched a program to help children develop a love of reading. She was inspired to set up the scheme by her father, who never learned to read and write. Dolly's Imagination Library sends free books to children aged 0–5 around the world, making Dolly a storytelling fairy godmother!

☆ INGREDIENTS ☆

250g (8oz) cherry tomatoes, halved
100g (3½ oz) pitted black olives
2 tablespoons capers in brine, drained
4 thyme sprigs, plus extra for garnish
4 cod fillets, about 17g (6oz) each
2 tablespoons extra virgin olive oil
2 tablespoons balsamic vinegar
salt and black pepper

☆ METHOD ☆

1. Combine the tomatoes, olives, capers and thyme sprigs in a roasting tin. Nestle the cod fillets in the pan, drizzle over the oil and balsamic vinegar and season to taste with salt and pepper.
2. Bake in a preheated oven, 200°C (400°F), Gas Mark 6, for 15 minutes.
3. Transfer the fish, tomatoes and olives to warmed plates. Spoon the pan juices over the fish. Serve immediately with a mixed green leaf salad or green vegetables.

She Never Met A POTATO (She Didn't Like)

SERVES 4 | PREP: 10mins | COOKING TIME: 20mins

"Every diet I've ever fell off it's been because of a potato, either French fries or mashed potatoes or baked potatoes. I never met a spud I didn't like." Just when the world thought Dolly couldn't be any more relatable, she revealed her passion for the humble potato! These no-waste recipes make the most of just six large spuds, Cheddar cheese and some store-cupboard spices for a carb-friendly feast that will have you kicking up your heels with Dolly-levels of happiness!

Potato Skins

☆ INGREDIENTS ☆

6 large potatoes, baked and cooled

150g (5oz) Cheddar cheese, grated

spray oil

chives, chopped, to garnish

☆ METHOD ☆

1. Cut the potatoes into quarters. Scoop out the potato flesh (use for the potato cakes). Transfer the skins to a bowl and spray with a little oil.
2. Cook the skins flesh-side down on the barbecue or under a hot grill for 2 minutes, turn and carefully sprinkle a little cheese on to each skin. Cook for a further 2 minutes until the cheese is melted.

Potato Cakes

☆ INGREDIENTS ☆

6 large potatoes, flesh roughly mashed

175g (6oz) Cheddar cheese, finely diced

1–2 teaspoon cumin seeds

2 teaspoons smoked paprika

4 tablespoons plain flour

salt and pepper

oil, for shallow-frying

☆ METHOD ☆

1. Combine the potatoes with the cheese, cumin seeds and paprika.
2. Divide the potato mixture into 12 pieces, shape each piece into a ball, then flatten slightly and dip into flour which has been seasoned with salt and pepper to lightly coat both sides.
3. Heat a thin layer of oil in a large, heavy-based frying pan. Cook the potato cakes for about 8 minutes, turning occasionally, until crispy and golden brown.

Smoky Mountain BACON CHEESEBURGERS

SERVES 4 | PREP: 15mins, plus chilling

COOKING TIME: 15mins

What could be more American than a good, ol' fashioned burger? This cheeseburger has a surprise smoky kick thanks to its glazed bacon rashers. Dolly grew up in the Great Smoky Mountains of East Tennessee, so if you ever find yourself camping out there, why not cook this on your grill? Remember, if you're cooking outside, you only need to lightly char the meats to make your taste buds sing like a country superstar!

• FUN FACT •

Dolly's burger of choice comes straight from a well-known chain! "I like those Whoppers at Burger King. That's always been my favourite."

SMOKY MOUNTAIN BACON CHEESEBURGERS

☆ INGREDIENTS ☆

750g (1½ lb) rib eye steak, minced
1 onion, finely chopped
1 garlic clove, crushed
2 teaspoons chopped thyme
8 smoked bacon rashers
2 tablespoons smoky barbecue sauce
olive oil, for brushing

8 bacon rashers
125g (4oz) Cheddar cheese, sliced
4 burger buns, halved
4 large butter lettuce leaves
2 tomatoes, sliced
salt and black pepper

☆ METHOD ☆

1. Put the beef, onion, garlic, thyme and some salt and pepper in a bowl. Using your hands, work everything together until evenly combined. Shape into 4 patties. Chill for 30 minutes.
2. While the patties are chilling, arrange the bacon rashers on a grill rack. Put the rack onto a baking tray and place in a preheated oven, 180°C (350°F), Gas Mark 4, for 10 minutes. Brush the bacon rashers with the barbecue sauce and cook for a further 5–6 minutes, until the bacon is crisp. Set aside and cover.
3. Brush the patties with a little oil and grill for 5–6 minutes on each side until cooked through and browned on the outside. Top the burgers with cheese and return to the hot grill for 30 seconds until melted.
4. Meanwhile, toast the buns for 1 minute on the cut side.
5. To assemble, stack the bottom half of the burger bun with lettuce leaves, tomato slices, a cheeseburger and two slices of bacon. Serve with fries.

Dessert

Here You CRUMBLE AGAIN

SERVES 4 | PREP: 10mins | COOKING TIME: 25–30mins

Back in 1977, Dolly was worried that releasing 'Here You Come Again' would alienate her country music fans, but this sparkly yet heartfelt mid-tempo pop single won her new fans and kept the old ones happy at the same time. Now, this hot and cold dessert is going to wrap your heart around its little finger. So, here you go …

☆ INGREDIENTS ☆

10 plums, pitted and sliced
4 teaspoons caster sugar
juice of 1 orange
100g (3½ oz) butter
150g (5oz) plain flour
1 teaspoon ground cinnamon
50g (2oz) soft brown sugar
50g (2oz) chopped hazelnuts
ice cream, to serve

☆ METHOD ☆

1. Put the plums, caster sugar and orange juice in a saucepan and cook for 3 minutes or until starting to soften, then spoon into an ovenproof dish.
2. Melt the butter and mix together with the remaining ingredients. Crumble the mixture over the plums, breaking up any large clumps.
3. Bake in a preheated oven, 190°C (375°F), Gas Mark 5, for 20–25 minutes until the topping is crisp. Serve with plenty of ice cream.

Love Is Like A BUTTERFLY CAKE

MAKES 12 | PREP: 15mins, plus chilling

COOKING TIME: 20mins

The butterfly has been a symbol associated with Dolly Parton throughout her career. To Dolly, the butterfly represents freedom, beauty and gentleness, while her firm but fair business tactics led to her being nicknamed 'The Iron Butterfly'. (Proving that you should never underestimate a woman who knows her own worth!) Get your own little piece of butterfly inspiration by baking these melt-in-the-mouth cupcakes.

LOVE IS LIKE A BUTTERFLY CAKE

☆ INGREDIENTS ☆

FOR THE CUPCAKES

150g (5oz) lightly salted butter, softened

150g (5oz) caster sugar

3 eggs

1 teaspoon vanilla extract

175g (6oz) self-raising flour

FOR THE BUTTERCREAM

250g (8oz) lightly salted butter, softened

400g (5oz) icing sugar

2 teaspoons vanilla extract

2 tablespoons whipping cream

☆ METHOD ☆

1. Line a 12-section bun tray with paper cake cases or stand 12 silicone cases on a baking sheet.
2. Put the butter and sugar in a bowl and beat with a hand-held electric whisk for 1–2 minutes until creamy. Whisk in the eggs and vanilla extract, then gradually tip in the flour and mix well until combined. Whisk the mixture for a further 4–5 minutes.
3. Divide the cake mixture between the cases. Bake in a preheated oven, 180°C (350°F), Gas Mark 4, for 20 minutes or until risen and golden. Transfer to a wire rack to cool.
4. Beat the buttercream ingredients together until smooth, around 4–5 minutes. Then cut a round from the centre top of each cooled cake using a small, sharp knife. Cut each round in half.
5. Put the buttercream in a piping bag fitted with a star nozzle and pipe a swirl into the cavity of each cake, or swirl in the buttercream using a teaspoon.
6. Reposition the 2 halves of the rounds on each cake at a 45° angle so that they resemble butterfly wings.

Hard Candy

CHRISTMAS TREATS

SERVES 20 | PREP: 15mins | COOKING TIME: 25mins

The secret to making this traditional peppermint candy is to work fast and keep the mixture warm so that it doesn't get too hard to cut. Use any colouring you like and gift it to your nearest and dearest in glass jars tied with a bow, because, just like Dolly's stage costumes, there's no such thing as too much decoration!

☆ INGREDIENTS ☆

500g (1lb) granulated sugar
250ml (8fl oz) water
200ml (7fl oz) golden syrup (corn syrup)
½ teaspoon peppermint extract
½ teaspoon food colouring
3 tablespoons icing sugar

☆ METHOD ☆

1. Combine the sugar, water and golden syrup in a large, heavy bottomed saucepan. Stir over a low heat until the sugar has dissolved. Allow to cook gently over a low heat without stirring until the mixture reaches 150°C (300°F) when checked with a sugar thermometer.
2. Add the peppermint extract and food colouring. Stir gently to mix then pour into two lightly oiled baking tins. Keep one of the tins warm over a saucepan of hot water (don't let the water touch the pan).
3. As the candy in the other pan begins to cool, use kitchen scissors to cut it into 2.5cm (1 inch) strips. Snip these strips into rough pieces and drop them onto a greased baking tray.
4. Toss the pieces in some of the icing sugar. Repeat the process until all the hard candy is set and cut.

• FUN FACT •

Dolly's version of 'Hard Candy Christmas' reached number 8 in the US country chart in 1983, and has been covered by artists including Cyndi Lauper, LeAnn Rimes and Reba McEntire!

Islands In THE CREAM

MAKES 20 | PREP: 30 mins, plus cooling

COOKING TIME: 1¼ hours

Some things just work together better as a duet – like Dolly and Kenny Rogers, or bananas and meringue! This recipe combines the tastes of Dolly's favourite banana pudding with cream and toffee fudge sauce to really hit the sweet spot. Just like the karaoke classic this dessert was inspired by, it's sure to become a legend in your own kitchen!

• FUN FACT •

Dolly performed 'Islands in the Stream' to a record-breaking crowd of around 180,000 Glastonbury-goers in 2014 in the UK festival's Legends slot!

☆ INGREDIENTS ☆

butter, for greasing
3 egg whites
100g (3½ oz) light muscovado sugar
75g (3oz) caster sugar
1 small ripe banana
1 tablespoon lemon juice
150ml (¼ pint) double cream
4 tablespoons ready-made toffee fudge sauce

☆ METHOD ☆

1. Grease 2 baking sheets. Line with nonstick baking paper. Whisk the egg whites in a very clean bowl until stiffly peaking. Gradually whisk in the sugars, a teaspoonful at a time, until it has all been added. Whisk for a few minutes more until the mixture is thick and glossy.
2. Take a large teaspoonful of meringue and, using another spoon to scoop off the first spoon, drop it onto the baking sheet to make an oval-shaped meringue. Continue until the mixture is used: making 40 meringues.
3. Bake in a preheated oven, 110°C (225°F), Gas Mark ¼ for 1–1¼ hours or until meringues are firm and may be easily peeled off the paper. Leave to cool on the paper.
4. Mash the banana roughly with the lemon juice. Whip the cream until it forms soft peaks, then whisk in 2 tablespoons of the toffee fudge sauce. Combine with the banana, then use to sandwich the meringues together and arrange in paper cake cases. Drizzle with the remaining toffee fudge sauce and serve. Store unfilled meringues in an airtight tin for up to 3 days.

Best Little FREAKSHAKE In Texas

SERVES 1 | PREP: 10mins

They say everything is bigger in Texas, and this mega-milkshake – or 'freakshake' – sure proves this point! Much like Dolly, it demonstrates the perfect amount of excess and confirms there's no such thing as too much decoration. Use the Not So Dumb Blondies recipe on page 101 for the brownie if you prefer a lighter chocolate flavour.

• TOP TIP •

Swap in canned whipped cream and ready-made chocolate sauce for speed and ease.

☆ INGREDIENTS ☆

65g (2½ oz) dark chocolate
200ml (7fl oz) double cream
300g (10oz) chocolate ice cream
250ml (8fl oz) milk
1 scoop vanilla ice cream
1 chocolate brownie square, halved
200g (7oz) mini marshmallows
5–6 pretzels

☆ METHOD ☆

1. Melt the chocolate in a bowl over a pan of simmering water. Remove from the heat and whisk in 100ml (3½ oz) of the double cream to make a sauce.
2. Put the chocolate ice cream and milk in a blender and blitz to combine.
3. Whip the remaining double cream with a hand blender until it forms soft peaks. Transfer to a piping bag fitted with a star nozzle.
4. Pour streaks of the chocolate sauce down the inside of the glass. Drop one piece of the brownie into the bottom.
5. Pour in the chocolate milkshake then add the scoop of vanilla ice cream.
6. Push the pretzels around the sides of the ice cream, then pipe the whipped cream on top.
7. Decorate with the mini marshmallows and remaining brownie. Eat with a long spoon and drink with a wide straw!

In The Sweet PEANUT PIE

SERVES 4 | PREP: 20mins | COOKING TIME: 6–8mins

This heavenly pie leaves all of its options open to make for a customizable taste of the Southern states! Crush the biscuits with a rolling pin in a food bag, or pulse in a food processer until you have fine crumbs. You could mix in Oreo or bourbon biscuits for a chocolate pie crust option, and use any of your favourite chocolate, peanut or honeycomb confectionary to decorate.

IN THE SWEET PEANUT PIE

☆ INGREDIENTS ☆

FOR THE PIE CRUST

200g (7oz) digestive biscuits, finely crushed

1 tablespoon muscovado sugar

100g (3½ oz) unsalted butter, melted

FOR THE FILLING

250g (8oz) cream cheese

100g (3½ oz) icing sugar, plus 2 tablespoons

250g (8oz) smooth peanut butter

250g (8oz) double cream

1 teaspoon vanilla extract

50g (2oz) dark chocolate, grated, to decorate

☆ METHOD ☆

1. Mix the crushed biscuits, sugar and melted better in a bowl to combine. Press into the base and sides of a 23cm (9 inch) pie dish. Bake in a preheated oven, 180°C (350°F), Gas Mark 4, for 10–12 minutes. Set aside to cool.
2. Beat together the cream cheese, the 100g (3½ oz) of icing sugar and peanut butter for around 3 minutes until light and fluffy.
3. Whisk the double cream until it has increased in volume. Add the 2 tablespoons of icing sugar and vanilla extract and whip again until peaks form.
4. Fold the whipped cream into the peanut mixture and tip into the pie crust. Smooth the surface and sprinkle over the grated chocolate to decorate. Chill for at least 6 hours in the refrigerator before serving.

Applejack STRUDEL

SERVES 6 | PREP: 30mins, plus soaking

COOKING TIME: 30–35mins

The layers of light filo pastry, soft apples and warming cinnamon make this the perfect hot dessert for a chilly winter's evening. Take inspiration from Dolly's childhood and enjoy it sitting around the fire playing music with family and friends!

• FUN FACT •

Dolly learned the banjo when she was a young girl but finds it much harder to play when she's wearing her trademark long acrylic nails!

APPLEJACK STRUDEL

✯ INGREDIENTS ✯

100g (3½ oz) muscatel raisins

2 tablespoons brandy

750g (1½ lb) dessert apples, cut into small dice

75g (3oz) fresh white breadcrumbs

50g (2oz) soft light brown sugar

grated zest of 1 lemon

50g (2oz) pine nuts, toasted

1 teaspoon ground cinnamon, plus extra for dusting

12 sheets chilled filo pastry from a 200g (7oz) pack

a little flour, for dusting

65g (2½ oz) unsalted butter, melted

2 tablespoons icing sugar, for dusting

✯ METHOD ✯

1. Put the raisins in a bowl, cover with the brandy and soak for 2 hours.
2. Put the apples in a bowl and add the breadcrumbs, sugar, lemon rind, pine nuts, cinnamon and the raisins and their juices. Stir well.
3. Lay 2 sheets of the pastry on a lightly floured work surface, next to each other and overlapping by about 2.5cm (1 inch) to form a larger sheet of pastry. Brush with melted butter, then top with the remaining pastry, brushing each layer with a little butter.
4. Spread the apple mixture over the pastry, leaving a 5cm (2 inch) border. Fold the long sides over the filling. Brush with butter and roll up from a short side to form a cylinder shape.
5. Transfer to a baking sheet, brush with the remaining melted butter and bake in a preheated oven, 200°C (400°F), Gas Mark 6, for 30–35 minutes until lightly golden.
6. Combine the sifted icing sugar with a little extra cinnamon and dust the strudel. Serve hot with custard or whipped cream and leave to cool before transferring to a serving plate.

Not So Dumb BLONDIES

MAKES 15 | PREP: 20mins | COOKING TIME: 40mins

Philanthropist, cultural icon, Billboard's Greatest Country Singer of All Time, movie star, businesswoman, national treasure ... the list of accolades goes on and on, and one thing's for sure – you underestimate Dolly at your peril! These 'not so dumb blondies' are deceptively easy to make and extremely hard to turn down, so let's cook up some surprises!

NOT SO DUMB BLONDIES

☆ INGREDIENTS ☆

400g (13oz) white chocolate, chopped
7g (3oz) slightly salted butter
3 eggs
175g (6oz) light muscovado sugar
150g (5oz) self-raising flour
150g (5oz) hazelnuts or Brazil nuts, chopped

☆ METHOD ☆

1. Melt 100g (3½ oz) of the chocolate and the butter in a heatproof bowl set over a saucepan of gently simmering water (don't let the base of the bowl touch the water).
2. Beat the eggs and sugar in a separate bowl until light and foamy. Stir in the melted chocolate mixture. Tip in the flour, remaining chopped chocolate and the nuts and mix until just combined.
3. Spoon the mixture into a greased and lined 28 x 18cm (11 x 7 inch) shallow baking tin and level the surface. Bake in a preheated oven, 190°C (375°F), Gas Mark 5, for about 35 minutes or until deep golden and just firm to the touch.
4. Leave to cool in the tin, then transfer to a board and cut into 15 squares.

• DOLLY • SAYS

"I'm not offended by all the dumb blonde jokes because I know I'm not dumb … and I also know that I'm not blonde."

Walk Of Fame STAR COOKIES

MAKES 12–14 | PREP: 15mins, plus chilling

COOKING TIME: 10–12mins, plus cooling

When she was awarded her second Hollywood Walk of Fame star in 2018 (to go with the one she received in 1984), Dolly became the first woman in the 21st century to achieve two stars on this entertainment landmark. Let's celebrate with these sparkling star biscuits! Top tip: You only need to crush the clear sweets down into small chunks to fill the gap. Now, step on up and enjoy the rewards of your labour!

WALK OF FAME STAR COOKIES

☆ INGREDIENTS ☆

125g (4oz) butter

125g (4oz) golden caster sugar

1 teaspoon vanilla extract

175g (6oz) plain flour

1 tablespoon cocoa powder

1 large egg

1 egg yolk

clear sweets, crushed

☆ METHOD ☆

1. Blend the butter, sugar and vanilla extract in a food processor. Add the flour, cocoa powder, whole egg and yolk. Blend again until the mixture forms a ball. Knead the dough lightly until it is smooth. Wrap and chill for 30 minutes.
2. Roll out the dough between 2 sheets of baking paper until it is 2.5mm (⅛ inch) thick. Cut out star shapes using a star cutter. Reroll the trimmings to yield as many cookies as you can.
3. Use a smaller star cutter to cut out the centre of each star. Carefully sprinkle in some of the crushed sweets to fill around three quarters of the space.
4. Leave the cookies on the baking paper and slide the paper on to 2 firm baking sheets. Bake in a preheated oven, 180°C (350°F), Gas Mark 4, for 10–12 minutes until the biscuits are firm and golden and the candy has melted.
5. Cool for around 10 minutes, then transfer to a wire rack to cool completely.

Parton PEACH COBBLER

SERVES 6 | PREP: 15mins | COOKING TIME: 20mins

Peach is one of Dolly's favourite flavours, and at DollyFest in 2021, a cocktail called Peachy Keen was even invented in her honour. Like many households, Dolly's got a recipe of her own for Peach Cobbler but this classic comfort dessert – with added blueberries – is worth bringing to a whole new audience!

PARTON PEACH COBBLER

☆ INGREDIENTS ☆

12 ripe peaches, halved and stoned

150g (5oz) blueberries

2 tablespoons light muscovado sugar

1 teaspoon cinnamon

175g (6oz) self-raising flour, plus extra for dusting

50g (2oz) unsalted butter, diced

50g (2oz) caster sugar

12ml (4fl oz) buttermilk

milk, for brushing

☆ METHOD ☆

1. Place the peaches and blueberries in a 750ml (1¼ pint) ovenproof dish and sprinkle over the sugar and cinnamon.
2. Place the flour in a bowl, add the butter and rub in with your fingertips until the mixture resembles fine breadcrumbs. Stir in the caster sugar, then add the buttermilk a little at a time, to form a slightly sticky, soft dough.
3. Turn the dough out on to a lightly floured surface and pat out until it is 1cm (½ inch) thick. Cut out 8 rounds using a 6cm (2½ inch) cutter.
4. Arrange over the top of the fruit and brush with a little milk. Place in a preheated oven, 180°C (350°F), Gas Mark 4, for 20 minutes or until the scones are golden and the fruit is bubbling. Serve immediately.

• FUN FACT •

DollyFest was set up to celebrate Dolly's life and career through music, food and art. This cultural festival is now called Rhinestone Fest, and anyone who has been inspired by Dolly can take part!

Halos And CREAM HORNS

MAKES 8 | PREP: 25mins | COOKING TIME: 12mins

Give in to temptation and ask for forgiveness later because you're going to be tooting your own horn over these showstopping pastries containing saintly cherries and sinful cream! Time to polish your halo and get baking, because these sweet treats are going to bring down the house!

HALOS AND CREAM HORNS

☆ INGREDIENTS ☆

butter, for greasing
200g (7oz) chilled puff pastry
flour, for dusting
beaten egg, to glaze
3 tablespoons granulated sugar
125g (4oz) pitted cherries
150ml (5fl oz) double cream
50g (2oz) vanilla sugar

☆ METHOD ☆

1. Grease 8 cream horn moulds with butter and line a baking sheet with nonstick baking paper. Roll out the pastry on a floured surface to about 40 x 12cm (16 x 5 inches) and cut into 8 long strips, then wind 1 strip around a mould, starting at the thin end and overlapping slightly, leaving a gap at the wide end. Place on the prepared baking sheet, cover and chill. Repeat with the remaining pastry strips.
2. Brush the pastry with beaten egg and sprinkle over the granulated sugar. Bake in a preheated oven, 200°C (400°F), Gas Mark 6, for 12 minutes, or until puffed and golden. Transfer to a wire rack to cool.
3. Meanwhile, reserve 8 of the cherries, then roughly chop the remainder. Whip the cream and vanilla sugar in a bowl with a hand-held electric whisk until thick, then fold in the chopped cherries.
4. Carefully twist the moulds from the cooled pastry, then place 1 reserved cherry in the bottom of each cone. Spoon in the cherry cream and serve immediately.

• FUN FACT •

Halos and Horns was the title of a TV show that Dolly pitched a couple of years before the album of the same name was released. It was never produced, so their loss is our gain!

I Am A
RAINBOW CAKE

SERVES 12 | PREP: 25mins | COOKING TIME: 15–20mins

This recipe uses the ingredients and method for the butterfly cakes on page 89, but with three times the amount of each ingredient. Make the cake mixture by following the instructions up to the end of Step 2, then use the instructions on the next page to complete the cake. Once it's ready, get set to take a bow once you reveal the rainbow within!

• FUN FACT •

Dolly's picture book *I Am a Rainbow* was written to help children learn how to express their feelings and emotions.

☆ INGREDIENTS ☆

FOR THE CAKES

Make three batches of the butterfly cake mixture from page 89.

FOR THE FROSTING

1 teaspoon vanilla extract

750g (1½ lb) cream cheese

325g (11oz) icing sugar

☆ METHOD ☆

1. Divide each batch of cake mixture into 2 bowls and colour each with 2–3 drops of food colouring. Stir well to mix. (You will end up with 6 differently coloured batches of batter.)
2. Tip each batch of cake mix into a 20cm (8 inch) round tin and bake in pairs on the same oven shelf for 15–20 minutes until slightly risen and a skewer inserted into the centre of the cake comes out dry. Turn out onto a cooling rack.
3. Make the frosting by briefly beating the vanilla essence into the cream cheese. Gradually add and combine the icing sugar, taking care not to over-mix or the frosting could split.
4. To assemble, place the purple cake on a cake stand or board and apply a layer of buttercream across the top. Carefully place the blue cake on the top and repeat with the buttercream and cake layers through green, yellow, orange and red. Use the remaining buttercream to apply a thin coating to the sides and top of the cake. Decorate as preferred.

Country Queen Of PUDDINGS

SERVES 6 | PREP: 25mins, plus standing

COOKING TIME: 35–45mins

Queen of Puddings is a traditional English dessert where breadcrumbs are soaked in a custard base and topped with jam and meringue. Sounds like a pudding fit for Country Royalty! Dolly has long been considered the Queen of Country Music and has encouraged subsequent generations of women songwriters and performers to make their voices heard in this genre, including Reba McEntire, Shania Twain, Emmylou Harris and Taylor Swift. Long live the Queen!

COUNTRY QUEEN OF PUDDINGS

☆ INGREDIENTS ☆

600ml (1 pint) milk
grated zest of 2 lemons
50g (2oz) unsalted butter
175g (6oz) caster sugar
10g (3½ oz) fresh breadcrumbs
4 eggs, separated
4 tablespoons apricot jam
125g (4oz) dried apricots, diced

☆ METHOD ☆

1. Pour the milk into a saucepan, add the lemon zest and bring just to the boil. Take off the heat and stir in the butter and 50g (2oz) of the sugar until the butter has melted and the sugar dissolved. Mix in the breadcrumbs and leave to stand for 15 minutes.
2. Mix the egg yolks into the milk mixture, then pour into a greased 1.5 litre (2½ pint) ovenproof pie dish. Bake in a preheated oven, 180°C (350°F), Gas Mark 4, for 20–25 minutes until the custard has set and is just beginning to brown around the edges.
3. Dot the jam over the baked custard and sprinkle with the diced apricots. Whisk the egg whites in a large bowl until stiffly peaking, then gradually whisk in the remaining sugar a teaspoonful at a time until thick and glossy. Spoon over the jam, then swirl with the back of the spoon.
4. Put the dish back in the oven for 15–20 minutes until the meringue is golden and cooked through. Serve warm with cream.

Berry PIES

SERVES 12 | PREP: 40mins | COOKING TIME: 30–35mins

No need to be shy – this yum-diddly berry pie will make you the apple of everyone's eye! If you prefer the flavour of just blackcurrants, use these in place of the redcurrants. Reroll the pastry trimmings to maximise the amount you have to work with and use any pretty l'il cutter to stamp a shape on the top of each pie.

• FUN FACT •

Dolly sometimes incorporates what she calls a form of 'country yodel' when singing different songs, including 'Berry Pie'.

☆ INGREDIENTS ☆

400g (13oz) mixed redcurrants and blackcurrants

2 tablespoons water

150g (5oz) caster sugar, plus extra for sprinkling

1 tablespoon cornflour

175g (6oz) raspberries

200g (7oz) small strawberries, quartered

500g (1lb) ready-made shortcrust pastry

milk, to glaze

☆ METHOD ☆

1. Cook the currants with the water and sugar in a saucepan for 5 minutes, stirring until soft. Mix the cornflour with a little extra water to make a smooth paste, then stir into the fruit and cook until thickened. Add the raspberries and strawberries, stir gently together, then leave to cool.
2. Reserve one-third of the pastry, then roll out the remainder thinly on a lightly floured surface. Stamp out 12 × 10cm (4 inch) circles with a fluted biscuit cutter and press into a buttered 12-section muffin tin.
3. Spoon the cooked fruit into the pies. Roll out the reserved pastry and cut out 12 × 7cm (3 inch) lids with a fluted biscuit cutter. Use another cutter to stamp a shape to decorate the centre of each pie top. Brush the top edges of the pies with a little milk, add the pastry lids and press the edges together well to seal.
4. Brush the pies with a little milk and sprinkle with sugar. Bake in a preheated oven, 180°C (350°F), Gas Mark 4, for 25–30 minutes until golden. Leave to stand in the tins for 20 minutes before serving warm with cream.

Drinks

White Limozeen LEMONADE

SERVES 6 | PREP: 5mins

This pineapple lemonade is a refreshing treat after a long day of running errands. You may not have been driving around town in a limo, but this will put you right back on your feet again. For a glitzy alcoholic version, add a shot of vanilla-flavoured vodka to your glass. Cheers!

• FUN FACT •

The White Limozeen rooftop bar in Nashville was named after Dolly's 1989 album and features all-pink décor in homage to our Country Music Queen!

WHITE LIMOZEEN LEMONADE

☆ INGREDIENTS ☆

250ml (8fl oz) lemon juice

500ml (17fl oz) pineapple juice

250ml (8fl oz) simple syrup, to taste

500ml (17fl oz) still or sparkling water, chilled

ice, to serve

lemon slices, to decorate

pineapple slices, to decorate

FOR THE SIMPLE SYRUP

250ml (8fl oz) water

250g (8oz) granulated sugar

☆ METHOD ☆

To make the simple syrup, combine the sugar and water in a small saucepan and allow to bubble gently over a medium heat until the sugar has dissolved. Allow to cool and store in the refrigerator in an airtight container for up to 1 month.

1. Pour the lemon juice and pineapple juice into a tall jug.
2. Stir gently to combine.
3. Check the flavour as you add the simple syrup until the lemonade is as sweet as you would like.
4. Add the cold water until the drink reaches your ideal strength and sweetness.
5. Pour into glass mugs or tall glasses, add ice and decorate with a lemon slice and pineapple wedge.

Steel Magnolia SPRITZ

SERVES 2 | PREP: 5mins

In 2024, Dolly launched a pretty ol' pair of drinks – Dolly Wines rosé and Dolly Wines prosecco. Either of these make the perfect ingredient for this light-as-a-butterfly version of a Hugo spritz. If you go for the rosé wine option, you'll get a pretty pink spritz. Use any rosé (pink) prosecco to achieve a sparkling cocktail otherwise.

STEEL MAGNOLIA SPRITZ

☆ INGREDIENTS ☆

½ cup ice cubes

50ml (2fl oz) elderflower liqueur, such as St-Germain

3–4 mint leaves

75ml (3fl oz) rosé prosecco or rosé wine

75ml (3fl oz) soda water or elderflower pressé

mint sprig, to decorate

lime wedge, to decorate

☆ METHOD ☆

1. Drop the ice cubes into a large wine glass.
2. Add the elderflower liqueur and mint leaves.
3. Pour over the prosecco or wine, along with the soda water or pressé.
4. Stir gently with a long metal spoon to mix the ingredients.
5. Decorate with the mint sprig and lime wedge.

• FUN FACT •

While filming the movie *Steel Magnolias* (1989) in Natchitoches, Louisiana, Dolly performed in a halftime show at a local college football game!

Imagin-Ger · MOJITO ·

SERVES 8 | PREP: 10mins, plus 1+ hours cooling

Once upon a time, a child-friendly mocktail was invented which was based on the classic mojito. Instead of lime, it used tastebud-tingling ginger! Use your imagination with the mixer and replace the ginger beer with lemonade for a more subtle flavour. (For adult mojito drinkers, include 200ml (7fl oz) of white rum at Step 1).

• FUN FACT •

Dolly Parton's Imagination Library reading program has gifted over 200 million free books to children around the world since 1995. A book is mailed out every 1.3 seconds!

IMAGIN-GER MOJITO

☆ INGREDIENTS ☆

75ml (3fl oz) ginger simple syrup

150ml (5fl oz) fresh lime juice

50g (2oz) mint leaves

500ml (17fl oz) ginger beer

soda water, chilled

ice cubes, to serve

mint sprigs, to decorate

ginger slices, to decorate

FOR THE GINGER SIMPLE SYRUP

75ml (3fl oz) water

75g (3oz) granulated sugar

50g (2oz) fresh ginger root, finely chopped

☆ METHOD ☆

To make the ginger simple syrup, combine the sugar and water in a small saucepan and allow to bubble gently over a medium heat until the sugar has dissolved. Add the ginger and leave to cool while the flavours infuse, for 1–24 hours and store in the refrigerator in an airtight container for up to 1 month.

1. Put the ginger syrup, lime juice and mint leaves into a tall serving jug. Mix well.
2. Pour over the ginger beer and stir to combine.
3. Top up the jug with soda water and stir again.
4. Pour into glasses half-filled with ice. Decorate with a sprig of mint and a slice of ginger.

Rockstar MARTINI

SERVES 2 | PREP: 5mins

This variant on the Rockstar martini (itself the younger sister of the Pornstar Martini) is made with Dolly's favourite fruit – peach! Play around with the flavours by swapping in bourbon, white rum or vanilla vodka, or use a different fruit liqueur until you've crafted the cocktail combination of dreams!

☆ INGREDIENTS ☆

50ml (2fl oz) whiskey
25ml (3fl oz) peach liqueur
25ml (1fl oz) vanilla syrup
25ml (1fl oz) fresh lime juice
Sparkling wine or Champagne
1 passionfruit, halved (optional)

☆ METHOD ☆

1. Pour the whiskey, peach liqueur, vanilla syrup and lime juice into a cocktail shaker filled with ice.
2. Shake well for around 30 seconds, or until the outside of the shaker is cold.
3. Strain into a coupe glass.
4. Decorate with a halved passionfruit (optional).

• FUN FACT •

Dolly's 2023 *Rockstar* album features guest appearances from over 40 music legends, including Paul McCartney, Sting, Joan Jett and Stevie Nicks!

Moonshiner MULE

SERVES 1 | PREP: 5mins

Although she has said that her mama didn't like when her daddy made moonshine (an illicitly distilled alcohol) himself, the tragic tale she tells on this topic in 'Daddy's Moonshine Still', ended up being one of her father's favourites. Thankfully, there's nothing heartbreaking about this very legal version of a Moscow Mule!

MOONSHINER MULE

☆ INGREDIENTS ☆

1 cup of ice
50ml (2fl oz) vodka
1½ teaspoon lime juice
125ml (4fl oz) ginger beer
mint sprig, to decorate
lime wedge, to decorate

☆ METHOD ☆

1. Put the ice into a metal mug or chilled glass.
2. Pour over the vodka and lime juice.
3. Top with the ginger beer and stir gently to mix.
4. Decorate with the mint sprig and lime wedge.

The Little SPARROW

SERVES 1 | PREP: 5mins

Dolly used the nickname 'Little Sparrow' as the title of her 2001 bluegrass album, which was dedicated to her father, Lee Parton, who called her "his little songbird". It was Dolly's 38th studio album and took her back to her bluegrass and Appalachian musical roots. This apple-based cocktail has a deep flavour and rich, smooth notes that needs to be sipped slowly to be appreciated. Here's to you, little sparrows.

THE LITTLE SPARROW

☆ INGREDIENTS ☆

50ml (2fl oz) Calvados

25ml (1fl oz) sweet vermouth

15ml (½ fl oz) Elderflower liqueur, such as St Germain

15ml (½ fl oz) apple brandy

1 teaspoon Peychaud's Bitters

apple peel or lemon twist, to decorate*

☆ METHOD ☆

1. Pour all of the liquids into a glass or cocktail shaker filled with ice.
2. Stir to combine.
3. Strain into a coupe glass.
4. Decorate with an apple peel or lemon twist.*

* To make fruit peel twists, take a strip of peel and wrap or roll it around a metal straw or chopstick. Carefully slide the twist off and lay over the rim of the glass.

A Cup Of
AMBITION

SERVES 1 | PREP: 5mins

Sangria is a traditional Spanish and Portuguese drink, much like an alcoholic fruit punch, which has a red or white wine base. In honour of Dolly's own favourite tipple – a glass of red wine – this is the red version. If you want to make a white sangria, change the mixture of chopped fruits to pear, peach and apple.

• FUN FACT •

The line "a cup of ambition" from Dolly's global hit, '9 to 5', has become a motivational phrase that inspires people to make their own dreams come true!

☆ INGREDIENTS ☆

750ml (1¼ pints) dry red wine, Spanish if possible

50ml (2fl oz) VSOP Cognac or good quality brandy

150ml (5fl oz) orange juice

3 tablespoons brown sugar

1 apple, cubed

1 orange, cut into halved segments

Ice, to serve

orange slices, to decorate

☆ METHOD ☆

1. Combine the wine, brandy, and orange juice in a tall jug.
2. Add the brown sugar and stir until dissolved.
3. Add the chopped apple and orange to the jug and leave to infuse for a minimum of 30 minutes (or overnight).
4. Serve chilled, over ice. Top up your glass with sparkling water for a softer flavour. Decorate with an orange slice, or any other soft fruit such as strawberry or peach.

To Know Gin Is To LOVE GIN

SERVES 6 | PREP: 15mins

What could be more Southern than a glass of iced tea? Not to be confused with sweet tea, or as Dolly's character in *Steel Magnolias* called it, "the house wine of the South", this alcoholic tea-infused drink uses pink gin and spiced rum to make the end of the working day taste even better (without the high sugar content). Cheers to all the pink drink lovers out there!

☆ INGREDIENTS ☆

1 chamomile teabag
500ml (17fl oz) boiling water
125ml (4fl oz) pink gin
125ml (4fl oz) spiced rum
125ml (4fl oz) elderflower cordial
175ml (6fl oz) pink grapefruit juice
2 cups of ice
3–4 rosemary sprigs, plus extra for decorating

☆ METHOD ☆

1. Pour the boiling water over the chamomile teabag in a heat-proof jug or bowl, and steep for 3–5 minutes. Remove the teabag and leave the tea to cool for 10 minutes.
2. Pour the tea into a large jug and add the gin, rum, elderflower cordial and pink grapefruit juice.
3. Stir in the ice and add 3–4 rosemary sprigs. Serve immediately, with an additional rosemary sprig in each glass.

Evening SHADE

SERVES 2 | PREP: 5mins, plus freezing

While Dolly sang of an unsympathetic home for young delinquents called evening shade, this recipe takes its cue from the sundowner colours of these fruit drinks instead – meaning there'll be no need to burn it all down! Experiment with your choice of wine and soft fruits or berries when making these slushies. There are two methods given to accommodate fresh or frozen fruit options on the next page.

• FUN FACT •

'Evening Shade' came from Dolly's fourth album, *My Blue Ridge Mountain Boy* (1969) and its cover showed a rare photo of her husband, Carl Dean.

Frozen Fruits Evening Shade

★ INGREDIENTS ★

400g (13oz) frozen strawberries or mixed berries

300ml (10fl oz) sparkling white wine

125ml (4fl oz) simple syrup (see page 117)

fresh berries, to decorate (optional)

★ METHOD ★

1. Tip the berries, wine and simple syrup into a blender. Blitz to a slushie pulp, approximately 10–20 seconds.
2. Serve immediately in a chilled glass, topped with fresh berries if using.

Fresh Fruits Evening Shade

★ INGREDIENTS ★

750ml (1¼ pints) bottle of red wine

400g (13oz) fresh cherries or mixed berries, such as strawberries and blackberries, 4 reserved to decorate

vanilla extract or honey, to taste

★ METHOD ★

1. Freeze the red wine in an ice cube tray for a minimum of 4 hours.
2. Tip the wine ice cubes and fruit into a blender. Blitz to a slushie pulp, approximately 10 seconds.
3. Add a dash of vanilla extract or honey. Taste to check the sweetness and blend again for 5 seconds to combine.
4. Serve immediately in a chilled glass, topped with fresh berries if using.

Bittersweet WHISKEY COFFEE

SERVES 2 | PREP: 6mins

What could be more comforting on a cold winter's night than an Irish coffee with an old friend? The bitterness of the black coffee is tempered by the sweetness of the cream and whiskey. This bittersweet combination is also the name of a 2023 song from Dolly's 'Rockstar' album, featuring Michael MacDonald. Many songs in the Appalachian bluegrass tradition also take their influence from Irish music, so this really is a match made in Dolly heaven.

BITTERSWEET WHISKEY COFFEE

★ INGREDIENTS ★

500ml (17fl oz) strong black filter coffee, hot

4 teaspoons brown sugar

50ml (2fl oz) Irish whiskey

50ml (2fl oz) whipping or double cream, cold

★ METHOD ★

1. Fill two coffee glasses with boiling water. Allow the glasses to heat up for up to 1 minute, then carefully pour away the water.
2. Put 2 teaspoons of sugar in each glass and add the hot coffee and whiskey. Stir until the sugar is dissolved.
3. Float half the cold cream over the coffee by slowly pouring it over the back of a spoon held over the glass.
4. Serve immediately and drink the coffee through the cream layer without mixing.

Alabama SUNDOWNERS

SERVES 1 | PREP: 5mins

'Alabama Sundown' was first recorded by Dolly Parton in 1971, and released on her album, *Bubbling Over* in 1973. In the lyrics, she reminisces about wanting to see an Alabama sundown while in New York in a cold December day. No matter where you hail from, there's nothing quite like a sundowner as the working day comes to an end. These golden-toned drinks will warm your soul and ease you into the evening. Kick back, put on this classic Dolly track, and enjoy.

Pimms Sundowner

☆ INGREDIENTS ☆

25ml (1fl oz) Pimms No 1

75ml (3fl oz) fresh apple juice

75ml (3fl oz) fresh orange juice

200ml (7fl oz) lemonade

ice cubes, to serve

orange slice, to decorate

☆ METHOD ☆

1. Drop 6–7 ice cubes into a large tumbler or glass jar.
2. Pour in the Pimms, fruit juices and lemonade.
3. Stir briskly.
4. Decorate with an orange slice.

Citrus Sundowner

☆ INGREDIENTS ☆

25ml (1fl oz) Grand Marnier (or similar orange cognac liqueur)

50ml (2fl oz) Southern Comfort (or similar whiskey liqueur)

75ml (3fl oz) white wine, such as Sauvignon Blanc, chilled

ice cubes, to serve

mint sprig, to decorate

☆ METHOD ☆

1. Drop 5–6 ice cubes into a cocktail shaker.
2. Pour in the liqueurs and white wine.
3. Shake for 30–40 seconds.
4. Strain into an ice-filled Old-fashioned glass.
5. Decorate with a mint sprig.

RECIPE NOTES

RECIPE NOTES

RECIPE NOTES

RECIPE NOTES

☆ INDEX ☆

INDEX